HOW TO READ A FINANCIAL REPORT

HOW TO READ A

WRINGING CASH FLOW AND OTHER

Second Edition

JOHN WILEY & SONS

NEW YORK CHICHESTER BRISBANE

FINANCIAL REPORT

VITAL SIGNS OUT OF THE NUMBERS

JOHN A. TRACY CPA

TORONTO SINGAPORE

This publication is designed to provide accurate and authoritative information in regard to the subject matter covered. It is sold with the understanding that the publisher is not engaged in rendering legal, accounting, or other professional service. If legal advice or other expert assistance is required, the services of a competent professional person should be sought. *From a Declaration of Principles jointly adopted by a Committee of the American Bar Association and a Committee of Publishers.*

Library of Congress Cataloging in Publication Data:

Tracy, John A.
  How to read a financial report.

  Includes index.
  1. Financial statements. I. Title.

HF5681.B2T733 1983   657'.33   83-6591
ISBN 0-471-88859-1
    0-471-83446-7 (Paperback)

Printed in the United States of America

10 9 8

PREFACE

I'm tempted to take all the credit for the success of the first edition. To be honest, however, I had superb editors and the publisher produced a handsome book. So my thanks go to John Wiley & Sons, and deepest appreciation to Gordon Laing and Richard Lynch. I could ask for no better editors. Also, I'm most grateful for the many favorable reviews of the first edition, from the *Chicago Tribune*, to *The Accounting Review*.

You may ask therefore: If the first edition has been such a good seller, why revise it? Recent developments in financial reporting, combined with the 1981 and 1982 changes in the income tax law, demand an updating of the book. This updating also provides the opportunity to make several improvements based on readers' comments and my experience in working with the book.

Most reviewers particularly like the centerpiece diagram in the first edition — the Master Exhibit that highlights the key connections among the basic financial statements. These cause-and-effect relationships are marked like highways on a roadmap. In this second edition the Master Exhibit has been extended to also show cash flow causes and effects. The name of the game today in business is cash flow, that's for sure.

Boulder, Colorado
June 1983

JOHN A. TRACY

PREFACE TO THE FIRST EDITION

Are you a business manager who needs a better understanding of the financial reports of your own company? Are you a banker or investor who wants better insight into the financial statements of other companies? Do you have doubts about the meaning of some items in financial reports? Are you not sure what to look for?

This book is for you.

You have an interest in financial reports, but neither the time nor the need for an in-depth knowledge of accounting. Therefore, this book contains no discussions of bookkeeping procedure, data processing, or maintaining accounting records. Just as you might explain football to a friend attending a game for the first time, this book tells you the "rules of the game" — the *basic* accounting rules — how those numbers in the financial statements were arrived at, and what they really mean.

Behind all the numbers is a simple, vital concept you must never lose sight of — *cash flow*. Business is run by keeping money moving. Financial statements report *where the money came from*, *where it's invested for the time being*, and, most important, *how often it has turned over*. Learning to gauge cash flow is one of the most important rewards you will get from this book.

Newspaper readers are accustomed to a quick read. Users of financial statements, in contrast, must settle for a slow read. They have to know which messages to look for, and which comparisons to make to get the messages. This book will teach you to read a financial report step by step. I've kept the number of steps to a minimum, and I make no unnecessary technical detours.

A word on accounting jargon: mastering a bit of accounting terminology is unavoidable if you want to understand financial statements. When a term is first introduced, it is carefully explained. But the way you master it is through repeated use. If at first you don't fully grasp a term, don't worry. Its meaning will become clear as we move along. By the end of the book you should have a good working knowledge of the language of accountants.

You'll look at a financial report with new awareness and new confidence in your ability to "unlock" the vital information it contains.

JOHN A. TRACY

Boulder, Colorado
October 1979

CONTENTS